FIRST NATIONS OF NORTH AMERICA

PLATEAU INDIANS

CHRISTIN DITCHFIELD

HEINEMANN LIBRARY
CHICAGO, ILLINOIS

H **www.heinemannraintree.com**
Visit our website to find out
more information about
Heinemann-Raintree books.

To order:

☏ Phone 888-454-2279

⌨ Visit www.heinemannraintree.com
to browse our catalog and order online.

© 2012 Heinemann Library
an imprint of Capstone Global Library, LLC
Chicago, Illinois

Original illustrations © Capstone Global Library, Ltd.
Illustrated by Mapping Specialists, Ltd.
Originated by Capstone Global Library, Ltd.
Printed in China by China Translation and Printing Services

14 13 12 11
10 9 8 7 6 5 4 3 2 1

Library of Congress Cataloging-in-Publication Data
Ditchfield, Christin.
 Plateau Indians / Christin Ditchfield.
   p. cm.—(First nations of North America)
 Includes bibliographical references and index.
 ISBN 978-1-4329-4951-8 (hc)—ISBN 978-1-4329-4962-4
(pb) 1. Indians of North America—Great Basin—Juvenile
literature. I. Title.
 E78.G67D57 2012
 979.004'97—dc22   2010040614

Acknowledgments

The author and publisher are grateful to the following for
permission to reproduce copyright material: Corbis: p. 18
(© Natalie Fobes); Getty Images: pp. 4 (© Marilyn Angel/
Nativestock.com), 20 (General Photographic Agency), 34
(MPI), 40 (© Marilyn Angel Wynn/Nativestock.com), 41 (©
Marilyn Angel Wynn/Nativestock.com); Library of Congress
Prints and Photographs Division: pp. 11, 13, 14, 16, 17, 19,
21, 25, 36; Nativestock.com: pp. 12 (© Marilyn Angel Wynn),
15 (© Marilyn Angel Wynn), 23 (© Marilyn Angel Wynn), 24
(© Marilyn Angel Wynn), 26 (© Marilyn Angel Wynn), 27
(© Marilyn Angel Wynn), 28 (© Marilyn Angel Wynn), 29
(© Marilyn Angel Wynn), 30 (© Marilyn Angel Wynn), 31
(© Marilyn Angel Wynn), 33 (© Marilyn Angel Wynn), 38
(© Marilyn Angel Wynn), 39 (© Marilyn Angel Wynn); The
Granger Collection, NYC: pp. 5, 35.

Cover photograph of beaded and painted deehide moccasins
reproduced with permission from the National Museum of the
American Indian (Smithsonian Institution/Walter Larrimore/
D229590).

We would like to thank Dr. Scott Stevens for his invaluable
help in the preparation of this book.

Every effort has been made to contact copyright holders of
any material reproduced in this book. Any omissions will
be rectified in subsequent printings if notice is given to
the publisher.

All the Internet addresses (URLs) given in this book were valid
at the time of going to press. However, due to the dynamic
nature of the Internet, some addresses may have changed, or
sites may have changed or ceased to exist since publication.
While the author and publisher regret any inconvenience this
may cause readers, no responsibility for any such changes can
be accepted by either the author or the publisher.

Contents

Some words are shown in bold **like this**. You can find out what they mean by looking in the glossary.

Who Were the First People in North America?

When the people of Europe first came to live in North America, they thought they had discovered a "New World." They didn't realize that this New World had already been discovered. It was already **inhabited** by millions of people, belonging to as many as 500 different **nations**. There are at least 3 million **descendants** of these first peoples still living in North America today.

Native American or American Indian?

In 1492 Christopher Columbus became the first European explorer to reach North America. He thought he had arrived in the Indies (South Asia), so he called the people he met "Indians." Although it soon became clear that Columbus had landed on a different **continent**, the native people continued to be called "Indians" for centuries.

▲ These riders are taking part in the Nez Perce Trail horse parade, a 1,170-mile (1,883-kilometer) ride that ends on the Bear Paw Battlefield in Montana.

▲ On August 3, 1492, Columbus and his crew set sail from Spain. They arrived in the New World five weeks later, on October 12.

In the 1960s, many native people began expressing their dislike for the name "Indian." Some said they should be known as Native Americans. (A native is a person who was born in a particular place.) Others preferred to be called American Indians, Natives, or First Peoples. Today all of these names are used to describe the race of people who have lived on the North American continent longer than anyone else. However, many people prefer to be known by their **tribe** or nation name, such as Nez Perce or Kutenai.

How Did the First People Come to North America?

Scientists believe that the first people to come to the North American **continent** came across land that connected North America to Asia. This is called the land bridge theory.

The land bridge theory

The Bering Strait is a waterway that runs between Russia and Alaska. Scientists believe it may once have been dry land, or that the water may have frozen during the **Ice Age**. Many thousands of years ago, people from Asia walked across this land bridge from one continent to another. They may have been hunting, following large herds of animals. They may have been looking for a new land with a better climate or more **natural resources**. These people and their **descendants** soon spread throughout North America, Central America, and eventually South America.

STORIES AND LEGENDS

Creation Stories

American Indians have many stories and legends about how their people came to live on the land. According to the Nez Perce legend, Coyote discovered that a giant monster was gobbling up all of his animal friends. Coyote jumped down the monster's throat and cut it to pieces with his knife, setting his animal friends free. He threw all the different pieces of the monster into the wind. Wherever the pieces landed, they turned into humans. These people became Coyote's new friends.

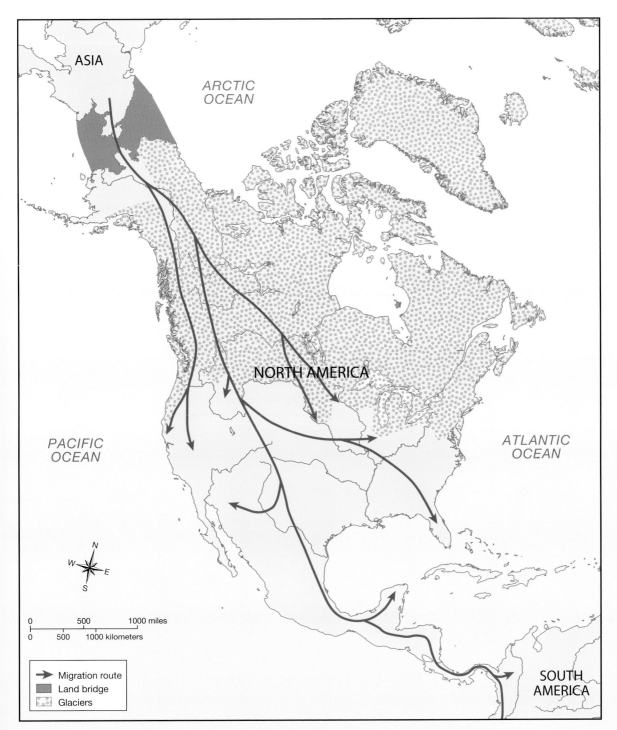

ASIA

ARCTIC
OCEAN

NORTH AMERICA

PACIFIC
OCEAN

ATLANTIC
OCEAN

N
W   E
S

0   500   1000 miles
0   500   1000 kilometers

Migration route
Land bridge
Glaciers

SOUTH
AMERICA

▲ This map shows how the first humans came to the Americas.

Tribes and nations

As the first people in North America spread out across the continent, they traveled in **clans** or family groups. Several clans living and working together formed **tribes**. Joining together with other tribes, they became **nations**.

Although at one time they were all related to each other, the tribes and nations living in different regions developed their own unique **characteristics**. They adapted, or changed, their way of life to fit their surroundings. They created their own languages, their own religious beliefs, and their own **culture** and **customs**. Tribes that lived near each other tended to be more alike than tribes living thousands of miles apart.

Anthropologists (scientists who study people groups) have identified 10 distinct groups of these peoples. These groups include—Arctic, California, Great Basin, Northeast, Northwest Coast, Plains, Plateau, Southwest, and Subarctic. Each of these groups is made up of many smaller, individual groups that share a similar way of life. This book is about the Plateau Indians.

LANGUAGE

Family Trees

One of the ways that anthropologists can tell which tribes are most closely related to each other is by studying their languages. Tribes that speak the same language or nearly the same language have probably come from the same part of the country. They most likely have common **ancestors** and come from the same family tree.

ARCTIC
OCEAN

Arctic

Subarctic

Northwest
Coast

Plateau

NORTH
AMERICA

PACIFIC
OCEAN

Plains

Northeast

ATLANTIC
OCEAN

Great Basin

California

Southeast

Southwest

Gulf of Mexico

N
W   E
S

0   500   1000 miles
0   500   1000 kilometers

▲ This map shows the different regions in which groups of American Indians share
similar characteristics.

Who Are the Plateau Indians?

There were once more than 50 individual American Indian **tribes** living between the Cascades and the Rocky mountains in the northwestern part of what is now the United States and Canada. This area is known as the Plateau region. Some tribes lived inland along the Columbia and Fraser rivers. Still others lived in the region that is now Idaho and Montana. These included the Flathead, the Nez Perce, and the Coeur D'Alene.

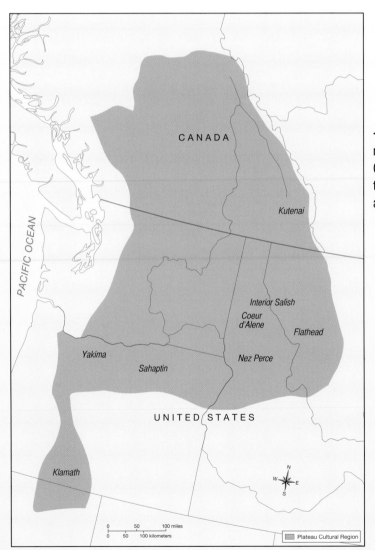

◄ The Plateau region covers parts of northwest United States and southwest Canada. This map shows where some tribes lived before European contact, and where some of them still live today.

Many Plateau Indian tribes lived at peace with one another. Members of one tribe married members of another. Their families remained closely related. Some tribes even formed **confederacies**. They formally declared themselves to be allies and friends. Other tribes were fierce enemies, often at war.

The Plateau Indians were famous for their skills as traders. They managed to acquire all kinds of things through their extensive trade with European explorers, American **settlers**, and other Indian tribes. The Plateau Indians sold them fish, seashells, animal furs, and even slaves—people who had been captured in conflicts between other tribes.

▶ This photo of a Klamath man in traditional dress was taken in 1923.

What Is the Plateau Like?

A plateau is a high, flat area of land. It is almost like a mountain with the top sliced off. The Northwest Plateau does have plenty of fields and flat land, but it also has thick, lush forests, tall mountains, deep canyons, and valleys. The western edge of the Plateau runs down to the Pacific Ocean, where the Northwest Coast Indians live. The southern edge borders the deserts of the Great Basin, a region of the country in which the rivers and lakes have no outlet to the sea. On every side, there are mountain ranges.

▲ This beautiful land is located near the National Bison Range on Flathead Indian **Reservation** in Montana.

▲ This is a photograph of a Nez Perce man coming to shore in a dugout canoe. It was taken in 1910.

The climate of the region varies, but there is always a lot of rain. Summers can be hot and humid, while winters are usually cold and snowy.

The Plateau region is rich in **natural resources**. It has many rivers full of fish to eat and fresh clean water to drink. Crops grow easily in the well-watered farmlands. The forests are almost like rainforests, bursting with many different kinds of plants, trees, and animals. Unlike Indians living in other parts of the country, the Plateau Indians did not have to struggle to survive from day to day. They had everything they needed to make a good life for themselves and their families.

How Did Early Plateau Indians Live?

The American Indians that lived in the Plateau adapted their way of life to both the climate and the **terrain**. Some lived in the forests. Some lived in the mountains or beside the rivers and lakes.

Homes and villages

In the summer, some Plateau Indians moved from place to place. They lived in homes called tipis. Tipis were tents made of grass mats, animal skins, or cloth stretched over long wooden poles. These cone-shaped homes could be put up or taken down very quickly, whenever the **tribe** decided to move on.

▲ Nez Perce Indians were living in the tipis in this photo in the early 1900s.

▲ A village of plank houses (also called lodges or longhouses) might house anywhere from 100 to 1,000 people.

Other Plateau Indians wove long, tough tule **reeds** (also called bulrushes) into mats. Twine or strips of leather were used to tie the mats together. These mats covered frames made of arched poles. This gave the homes a round shape. In the winter, these Plateau Indians dug pits that were 3 to 6 feet (about 1 to 2 meters) deep and 7 feet (more than 2 meters) across. They used the tule mats to build high-arching roofs over the top of the pits. The dirt walls made the pit houses much warmer inside. Bark lodges were also common among some Plateau Indians.

Some groups settled permanently in different regions of the Plateau. They built large wooden houses from cedar planks. These lodges or plank houses looked like long, narrow barns. Some were more than 70 feet (21 meters) long! Several families shared the same home.

Early Plateau Indian clothing

Early Plateau Indians made their own clothing from whatever materials they could find. In hot weather, they used green leaves, long grasses, and other plant fibers. They wove these fibers into breechcloths or aprons, with front and back flaps that hung from the waist. They also made reed capes to keep themselves dry during the rainy season. In cold weather, men wore shirts and leggings made of animal skins. They bundled up in warm robes made of animal fur.

The women wore short grass skirts or aprons in the summertime, just like the men. In the winter, they added leggings and fur coats. Later, the women of the Plateau wore long dresses with their leggings, similar to women of the Plains region. They traded with Europeans for cloth blankets to make coats and capes. Mothers carried their babies on their backs in carriers called cradleboards.

▶ This Nez Perce man is dressed for winter.

16

Hairstyles and shoes

Hairstyles depended on what was popular in a particular tribe. Most men and women wore their hair long and loose.

Both men and women wore shoes that were similar to **moccasins**—soft shoes make of animal skin. On special occasions, they decorated their bodies with paint, piercings, and tattoos. They also wore jewelry made of shell or bone, and basket hats made of spruce roots. Later they wore headdresses made of feathers, similar to the Plains Indians.

▲ Some cradleboards had wooden devices that gently applied pressure to a baby's soft skull, molding his or her head into a shape that Plateau Indians found attractive.

▲ A member of the Yakima tribe uses a traditional dip to catch Chinook salmon on the Klickitat River in Washington.

Finding food

The main source of food for the early Plateau Indians was salmon fishing. The rivers were full of these rich and nutritious fish. The Indians also caught trout, **smelt**, and eel.

The men hunted for deer, bison, bear, elk, and caribou. They used bows and arrows, spears, nets, or traps to catch and kill their **prey**.

The women gathered roots and nuts. They picked huckleberries, blueberries, and strawberries. They also picked wild vegetables, such as carrots and rice. They used these ingredients to make many kinds of cereals, soups, and stews.

Salmon

Some Plateau Indians believed that the salmon were once humans who came to Earth in human form. The salmon willingly gave up their lives so that others could live.

▲ This is a photograph of a Yakima woman gathering roots to use for food and medicine.

What Was Family Life Like for Early Plateau Indians?

Families usually consisted of one man, one woman, and their children. Sometimes two or three wives would share the same husband. Each member of the family played an important role. Men were responsible for protecting and providing for the family. Women took care of the home. Although only men were chiefs and tribal council leaders, women's opinions were respected. In matters of war, men took the lead. When it came to issues that impacted the family, women often made the important decisions.

▲ This photo shows members of a Flathead family outside their home.

Life of Early Plateau Indian Boys and Girls

Men taught young boys how to hunt and fish and how to fight to protect the **tribe** from its enemies. Women taught the young girls how to cook, sew, and take care of their homes. Everyone did their part.

On special occasions, a wealthy family would host a great feast. These feasts included all kinds of singing, dancing, and celebrating. In addition to a good meal, the guests were given gifts such as food, blankets, robes, and even canoes! In this way, those people who had more shared with those who had less.

◄ This Salish Indian boy wears a ceremonial costume and headdress.

21

Languages

In one sense, each of the more than 50 Plateau tribes had their own language, or their own **dialect** or accent. Words and phrases had a certain meaning to one tribe and a different meaning to another. However, a careful study of these languages reveals that they are actually very similar. They all fit into one of four larger language groups or families—the Kutenai family, the Interior Salishan family, the Sahaptin family, and the Modoc family.

Salishan Words	
English	**Salishan**
One	Nko'o
Two	Eseł
Three	Tsełe
Four	Mos
Five	Tsił
Man	Skaltamiax
Woman	Simmu'em
Sun	Spukani
Moon	Saka'am
Water	Se'ułku

▲ This chart shows some of the Salishan words spoken by Flathead Indians.

Kutenai Words	
English	**Kutenai**
One	Óke
Two	As
Three	Káhlssa
Four	Hátsa
Five	Yíku
Man	Titkat
Woman	Páhlki
Dog	Hálchin
Sun	Natánik
Moon	Natánik
Water	Wóo

▲ The Kutenai language is not related to any other known language.

▲ Plateau Indians traded items such as the tools above.

Trading

The early Plateau Indians did a lot of trading, not only with other tribes from the Plateau, but with tribes from the Plains. They also traded with Europeans, including explorers from England, France, and Russia.

What Did Early Plateau Indians Believe?

Many early Plateau Indians believed that the world was full of spirit beings. Every rock and tree, every mountain and lake, and every animal had a spirit. They also believed there were **supernatural** spirit beings that **inhabited** the sky and Earth. These spirits often intervened, or got involved, in people's lives. They guided and protected the people by giving them wisdom and pointing them to the truth. Other Plateau Indians shared a deep faith in a Creator, who blessed those who worked hard and lived responsibly. Some Plateau Indians carry on these beliefs today.

▲ A member of the Kutenai **tribe** chants a traditional prayer, while holding a talking stick decorated with an eagle claw.

Vision quests

Early Plateau Indians believed that everyone had a **guardian** spirit who guided him or her through life. These spirits most often took the form of animals or objects in nature. They gave people wealth and happiness. They also gave them special powers like strength or speed, skill in hunting, or the ability to heal the sick.

As they turned 12 or 13 years old, young boys and some girls were encouraged to go out alone on a vision quest. This was a time for them to connect with their guardian spirits and hear what the spirits might say to them. Once they returned to their village, they were treated as adults.

▶ This Klamath Indian chief stands on a mountain overlooking Crater Lake in Oregon.

Leaders

Both men and women could become spiritual leaders of their tribe. Spiritual leaders believed that they had been given the power to cure diseases. They cast evil spirits out of those who were sick or troubled and in distress. They also believed they could communicate with the supernatural spirit world and the spirits of the dead.

Stories and legends

Coyote appears in the myths and legends of many western Indian tribes. This beloved character is a mischievous trickster, always getting into trouble with the other spirits represented by the animal kingdom. According to some myths, whether by accident or on purpose, Coyote was responsible for the creation of people. The Plateau Indians tell many tales of Coyote's adventures.

▲ Spiritual leaders were greatly respected and even feared by other members of the tribe.

There are many other interesting stories and legends that are a part of American Indian **culture**. The Plateau Indians have stories about the creation of the world and the great flood. They have stories that explain the origin of people, plants, and animals. Many of the main characters in their stories are animals. There are also stories about powerful giants, skillful hunters, brave warriors, and beautiful **maidens.**

▲ According to Nez Perce legend, this rock formation was made by Coyote the Trickster. He threw his fishing net across the river in a fit of anger, and it turned to stone.

Celebrating life

Storytelling was such an important way for the early Plateau Indians to celebrate their culture and their way of life. Most tribes had no written language, so their children learned their tribal and family histories by listening to older people tell stories about the past.

Early Plateau Indians also celebrated their beliefs in their art, music, and dance. Plateau Indians were expert weavers. They used the tule **reeds**, as well as other long grasses to create clothing, baskets, and bags for carrying special objects. Women sewed amazing patterns and designs on their clothing. Men carved fancy details onto their tools and their children's toys. They made their own musical instruments, including drums, rattles, and flutes.

Dances were performed as part of their religious ceremonies. Each dance had its own special steps and movements. Children learned to do the dances by watching their parents and grandparents.

Early Plateau Indians found plenty of time to laugh and play. They enjoyed all kinds of games. They ran races, threw arrows at targets, and hid special objects for others to find. They also played a stick and ball game similar to field hockey. Modern Plateau Indians carry on many of these traditions today.

◄ Plateau women made baskets such as this one out of tule reeds.

Winter Ceremonies

During the summer, early Plateau Indians were able to store up more than enough food for the winter. So when winter came, they didn't have to go out and hunt to feed their families. They had time to plan **elaborate** dramas, music, and dances. The Winter Ceremonies were always the most exciting. Many Plateau Indians still hold these celebrations today.

▲ This father and son are performing a traditional dance together during the Bitteroot Valley Pow Wow near Hamilton, Montana. Dancers who dress in costumes such as these are sometimes known as "fancy dancers."

When Did the Plateau Indians First Use Horses?

Spanish explorers brought horses to North America in the 1500s. Some horses escaped into the wild, where Indians found them. Others were captured during conflicts with other **tribes**. By the 1700s, the Plains Indians had learned how to **breed** and train these animals. They traded them to other tribes, including the Plateau Indians. For the Plateau Indians, having horses changed everything.

How horses changed life for the Plateau Indians

Suddenly Indians could travel much farther and faster across the Plateau. They could hunt buffalo much more effectively. It was easier to circle the buffalo herds on horseback. Hunters could quickly move back and forth, swooping into and around the herd. Members of the Flathead, the Kutenai, the Coeur D'Alene, and the Nez Perce often went on hunting parties together.

◄ This Appaloosa horse is wearing a special saddle created by the Nez Perce. The pommels are used for hanging beaded bags, baskets, and baby carriers.

As they traveled more, many early Plateau Indians chose to live in tipis rather than the pit houses and lodges that their **ancestors** preferred. These tent-houses were easier to build and break down quickly. The traveling Indians now had more contact with Indians from other parts of the country—particularly the Plains Indians. The Plateau Indians started adopting the **culture** of the Plains Indians, adding Plains **customs**, traditions, and beliefs to their own. They even started wearing similar clothing and headdresses.

◄ In 1839 artist George Catlin drew this picture of two hunters sneaking up on a herd of bison on the Great Plains.

Plains Indians

As American **settlers** moved west, the Plains Indians were forced to move farther west to avoid conflict with them. Sometimes these tribes moved into Plateau Indian territory. The Plateau Indians moved even farther west to stay out of their way.

Which Explorers First Met the Plateau Indians?

For hundreds of years, the Indians lived peacefully on the Plateau. Aside from occasional contact with trappers and fur traders, they had little to do with non-Indian peoples. Then in 1803, President Thomas Jefferson completed the Louisiana Purchase.

For $15 million, Jefferson bought about 827,987 square miles (2,144,500 square kilometers) of land in North America from France. This new U.S. territory extended north from the Gulf of Mexico all the way to Canada, and west from the Mississippi River to the Rocky Mountains.

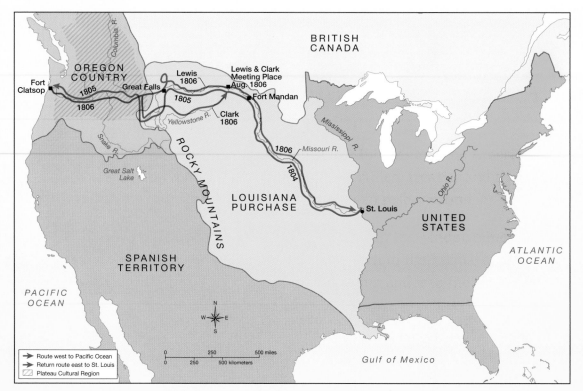

▲ This map shows the Louisiana Purchase, as well as the routes that Lewis and Clark took through the country.

In 1804 Jefferson sent a group of explorers led by Meriwether Lewis and William Clark to scout out the land. They would learn as much as they could about the territory and see if they could find a water route to the Pacific Ocean.

In the fall of 1805, Lewis and Clark reached the Pacific Ocean. There they met members of the Clatsop **tribe**. These Indians were very friendly and helpful to the explorers. They were eager to do business with them. In fact, the Clatsop urged the explorers to stay and spend the winter with them. Lewis and Clark agreed. They set up their camp and called it Fort Clatsop.

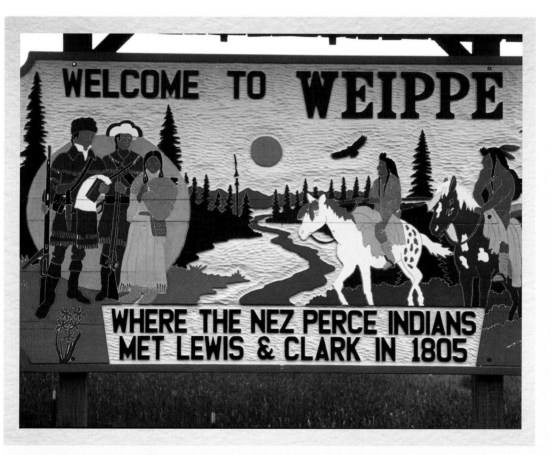

▲ This sign welcomes visitors to the Weippe Prairie, a national historic landmark in the Nez Perce National Historic Park in Idaho and Montana.

Learning to live together

Soon thousands of American **settlers** began moving west across the plains and into the Plateau region. These settlers brought with them all kinds of new things that the Plateau Indians had never seen before. They brought new weapons, new tools, fabrics, and other household items. Plateau Indians found that the settlers were eager to trade these items for things they needed.

At first the relationships were friendly and beneficial to both sides. Plateau Indians used the new weapons, tools, and technology to improve their lives. Many Plateau Indians learned to speak English, French, or Spanish. They also learned to read and write. This helped them create a written record of their own languages, **cultures**, and histories.

▲ In the 1850s, the artist William Henry Jackson was one of many American settlers traveling west. He later painted this scene from his journey on the Oregon Trail.

▲ This is a drawing of Fort Bridger, an important trading post located along the Green River in Black Forks, Wyoming, in 1857.

Missionaries

Christian **missionaries** came to share their faith with the Plateau Indians. Many Plateau Indians became Christians. Others took Christian teachings and combined them with their own traditional faith to create a blended religion that is still practiced by some Plateau Indians today.

Conflict and war

Unfortunately, the settlers also brought with them sickness and disease. These illnesses wiped out entire tribes. There were also constant conflicts and misunderstandings between the tribes and the settlers—particularly over who owned the land and who had the right to live there. When gold was discovered on tribal lands, it only made things worse. Now the U.S. government was anxious to take control of land that belonged to the Plateau Indians. Their disagreements often led to war.

Why Did the Plateau Indians Lose Their Lands?

Tension grew between the Plateau Indians and the new **settlers**. They fought over who owned the land, who had the right to live there, and whose laws and **customs** should be obeyed. **Treaties** were made and broken, time and time again. Sadly, the American Indians were outnumbered. Although they fought back fiercely, they could not hold onto their lands or their way of life.

▶ Chief Joseph became the last Indian chief to surrender to the U.S. Cavalry after evading capture for many years. He famously declared: "Hear me, my chiefs, I am tired. My heart is sick and sad. From where the sun now stands, I will fight no more forever."

Moving to the reservations

In the late 1800s, the U.S. government passed a series of laws forcing all American Indians to move onto **reservations**. These are specific areas of land set aside for American Indians.

The Plateau Indians had already lost their lands unofficially. Since the first explorers, thousands of people had moved in and forced them out. Some Indians had gone north into Canada. Others were wiped out by **famine**, disease, and war. Now they had no choice but to move onto the reservations and try to keep at least some of their traditions alive.

In the 1900s, after much debate and public protest, the unfair laws were changed. New, fairer policies were put into place. Unfortunately, for many Plateau Indians, it was too little, too late.

◄ Many American Indians were forced to move onto reservations established by the U.S. government.

Where Are the Plateau Indians Now?

Today many Plateau Indians still live in the northwestern United States and southwestern Canada. Many choose to live on **reservations** in Montana, Washington, Oregon, and California. There are about 2,700 members of the Nez Perce living on the **tribe's** reservation in Northern Idaho. Some live on Indian reserves in the Canadian provinces of Alberta and British Columbia. Others, however, choose to make their homes in towns and cities among people of all different races and **cultures**.

In many ways, they live just like other North Americans. They work as teachers, doctors, lawyers, and engineers. Some are artists, athletes, actors, and entertainers. Others work in ranching and fishing. Today's Plateau Indians operate campgrounds and tourist attractions. They own restaurants, hotels, casinos, and other businesses.

▲ A Nez Perce horse trainer works with an Appaloosa horse in Sweetwater, Idaho. The Nez Perce developed the Appaloosa **breed** hundreds of years ago. Horse breeding and training is still an important part of Nez Perce culture today.

Preserving their past

While living their modern lives, however, these Plateau Indians try to **preserve** the history and culture of their **ancestors**. They want their children to understand where they have come from and what it means to be an American Indian. Parents and grandparents work especially hard to pass on these traditions to the next **generation**.

▲ It is important to teach young American Indians the languages that their grandparents and great-grandparents used to speak. Otherwise these languages will soon become endangered or even **extinct**—and a part of their culture will be lost forever.

Staying connected

There are many books, magazines, and newspapers that celebrate the American Indian way of life. Museums and cultural centers display historical **artifacts**. They house samples of traditional fine arts, basketry, pottery, tools, instruments, jewelry, and clothing. New technology is also making it possible for Plateau Indians to preserve their past. Websites and online groups help them connect with one another to share their history and culture with the world.

Festivals and celebrations

There are two million American Indians living in the United States today. That's less than one percent of the country's population. Many still choose to live on one of the 314 reservations established by the U.S. government.

▲ A Nez Perce cradleboard and a pair of **moccasins** are beautifully decorated with traditional beadwork and designs.

Each year, hundreds of American Indians gather at Indian festivals across the country. They perform ceremonial songs and dances. They share traditional arts, crafts, and recipes. Rodeos and parades are often part of the festivities. By participating in these events, the American Indian peoples celebrate their past, present, and future.

▲ Nez Perce Indian Carla High Eagle is dressed in a traditional costume, riding an Appaloosa horse, for a special ceremony or celebration of Nez Perce history and culture.

Timeline

about 10,000 BCE	Groups of people come from Asia across the land bridge into North America. They are the first people to arrive in North America.
1492 CE	Explorer Christopher Columbus becomes the first European to "discover" the New World.
1700s	The Plateau Indians acquire horses in their trading with the Plains Indians.
1700s–1800s	Explorers from Europe and Asia sail across the Pacific Ocean and begin engaging the Plateau Indians in what becomes the Maritime Fur Trade.
1805	The Lewis and Clark Expedition encounters the Plateau Indians.
1830s	American **settlers** begin moving even farther west, into Plateau Indian territory.
1855	Conflict between the Plateau Indians and the American settlers leads to a series of worthless **treaties** and the forced removal of the Indians to **reservations**.
1872–1873	The Modoc War takes place when the Modoc **tribes** leave the reservations and return to their tribal lands. Ultimately they are forced to surrender to the U.S. Army.
1877	The Nez Perce War becomes the last great battle between the U.S. government and any Indian **nation**. Chief Joseph surrenders.
1881	Helen Hunt Jackson publishes a book called *A Century of Dishonor*, exposing the mistreatment of American Indians by the U.S. government.

1924   The Indian Citizenship Act extends citizenship and voting rights to all American Indians. (But not all Indians welcome this.)

1934   The Indian Reorganization Act returns American Indians' authority to self-govern and reverses some of the unfair government policies of the past.

1968   The American Indian Movement (AIM) organizes protests against the unfair treatment of American Indians and calls on the government to keep its promises to the people.

1990   Congress passes the Native American Languages Act, "to **preserve**, protect, and promote the rights and freedoms of all Native Americans to use, practice and develop Native American languages."

1990   On August 3, President George H.W. Bush proclaims the first National American Indian Heritage Month. President Clinton affirms this special designation in November of 1996.

2004   The National Museum of the American Indian is established on the National Mall in Washington, D.C.

Glossary

ancestor family member that lived a long time ago; great-grandparents, great great-grandparents, and so on

anthropologist scientist who studies the beliefs and ways of life of different people

artifact object belonging to or used by people of the past

breed produce a certain kind of animal or plant by human care

characteristic something that makes a person special or different from others

clan large group of families that are related to each other

confederacy group of people united by a common goal or cause

continent one of the seven large land masses of the Earth, including Asia, Africa, Europe, North America, South America, Australia, and Antarctica

culture group's beliefs, traditions, and way of life

custom usual way of doing things for a particular group of people

descendant children, grandchildren, great-grandchildren, and so on

dialect way a language is spoken by a particular group of people

elaborate very complicated and detailed

extinct something that has died out or no longer exists

famine great shortage of food

generation group of people born during a certain time

guardian someone who guards or protects another person

Ice Age period of time thousands of years ago, when Earth's climate was much colder and entire regions were covered by glaciers

inhabit live or dwell in

maiden young, unmarried woman

missionary person who travels to other places to share his or her faith and do good works

moccasins soft shoes made of animal skin

nation group of people who live in the same part of the world and share the same language, customs, and government

natural resources substances found in nature that have many important uses

preserve keep safe

prey animal that is hunted for food

reed tall, slender grass

reservation area of land set aside by the U.S. government as a place for American Indians to live

settler person who moves to a new place and builds a home there

smelt very small fish that live in seawater

supernatural out of the ordinary, beyond the laws of nature

tension unfriendliness between groups of people

terrain ground or land

tribe group of people who are related to each other and share the same laws, customs, and beliefs

Find Out More

Books

Dennis, Yvonne Wakim. *A Kid's Guide to Native American History: More Than 50 Activities*. Chicago: Chicago Review Press, 2010.

Doherty, Craig A. and Katherine M. Doherty. *Plateau Indians*. New York: Chelsea House, 2008.

Hopping, Lorraine Jean. *Chief Joseph: The Voice for Peace*. New York: Sterling, 2010.

Murdoch, David H. *North American Indian*. New York: DK Eyewitness Books, 2005.

Websites

Native American Facts for Kids
www.native-languages.org/kids.htm
This website provides simple information about American Indians in an easy-to-read question and answer format.

First People of America and Canada
www.firstpeople.us/
This is an educational site full of great information about American Indians and members of the First Nations.

DVDs

500 Nations. Directed by Jack Leustig. Warner Home Video, 2004.

A History of American Indian Achievement. Directed by Ron Meyer. Ambrose Video, 2008.

We Shall Remain: America Through Native Eyes. Directed by Chris Eyre and Sharon Grimberg. PBS, 2009

Places to visit

National Museum of the American Indian
Fourth Street and Independence Avenue SW
Washington, D.C.
www.nmai.si.edu/

George Gustav Heye Center
One Bowling Green
New York, NY
www.nmai.si.edu/subpage.cfm?subpage=visitor&second=ny

Nez Perce National Historical Park
Idaho, Montana, Oregon, and Washington
www.nps.gov/nepe/index.htm

Further research

What did you find to be the most interesting about the Plateau Indians?
How does early life for these people compare to the way you live today? You
can find out much more by visiting your local library or searching online.

Index